NEIL ENTWISTLE 'S DAY IN COURT

Michael Wells Glueck
Author, *Living Among The Swiss*
What I Learned At University
The Retirement Home Experience
The Trial Of Thomas E. Toolan III

Neil Entwistle's Day In Court

ISBN-10: 1-0862-1071-9
ISBN-13: 978-1-0862-1071-2

All Rights Reserved
Copyright 2008

No part of this book may be reproduced or transmitted in any form or by any means, graphic, electronic, or mechanical, including photocopying, recording, taping, or by any information storage or retrieval system, without written permission from the author or publisher.

Introduction

On January 22, 2006, during a follow-up visit by local police, the incipiently decomposing bodies of Rachel Entwistle and her nine month-old daughter Lillian Rose were discovered lying under a comforter in the master bed of their Hopkinton, Massachusetts home. Rachel lay on her left side, her right arm across her daughter's heart. They had been shot to death two days before with a twenty-two caliber revolver. In an act widely interpreted as a sign of guilt, the paterfamilias, Neil Entwistle, upon discovering their corpses, had fled to England on the following day after purchasing a one-way airline ticket, allegedly to be comforted by his parents, leaving the task of burial to Rachel's stepfather, Joseph Matterazzo of Carver, Massachusetts, the owner of the revolver. Neil wanted the pair buried together, Mr. Matterazzo eventually testified, because "that's how he had left them." Within three weeks, the police investigation of the murders led to Neil's arrest and, after extradition had been waived, to his escorted return to Massachusetts. Subsequent evidence-gathering and DNA-testing took time; seasoned defense attorneys in private practices of their own were appointed by the public defender's office; Entwistle finally stood in the dock nearly two and one-half years later, on June 2, 2008, having spent virtually all of that time (except for brief court appearances) in the Middlesex County jail.

If convicted of multiple first-degree murders, he faces life imprisonment without the possibility of parole; Massachusetts law does not provide for a death sentence. Inmates convicted of crimes against children generally do not fare well in American penitentiaries; Entwistle has already been kicked in the chest by another inmate at the Middlesex County jail. And the maximum-security institution to which he would likely be sent – Cedar Junction Prison in South Walpole, Massachusetts – is a much grimmer place, as was formerly attested in a currently non-functioning website, www.Shutdownddu.org/walpole.htm. (DDU stands for Departmental Disciplinary Unit.) After several years, if he survives, upon good behavior he may become eligible for transfer to a medium-security prison. A conviction for a lesser offense would carry a somewhat less onerous sentence (typically twenty-five years to life) with the possibility of parole. There would be an automatic appeal for a first-degree murder conviction, limited to matters of law rather than of fact. The likely grounds would be the trial judge's denial of a change of venue (please see page six); the probable outcome, affirmation of the verdict and sentence, as appeals of this nature are rarely successful. Prison sentences in the U.S. are far harsher than in Europe, where the penalty for an initial murder is typically ten to fifteen years' incarceration.

    The story of Rachel's meeting Neil at the British University of York's rowing club on the Foss and Ouse Rivers during her junior college year abroad, as well as of their developing relationship, romance, and marriage, is told in Michele R. McPhee's *Heartless: The True Story of Neil Entwistle and the Cold-Blooded Murder of his Wife and Child*, published on June 3, 2008 as a mass-market paperback by St. Martin's Press in its True Crime Library.

After initially living with the Matterazzos in Carver, the young, newly married couple leased a house in Hopkinton in the interests of privacy, especially while making love expressively, and in order to separate their dog, Sally, from their hosts' dog, Cassie, as the two animals did not get along well.

The focus of this book is upon the trial that began, as noted, on June 2, 2008, one day before publication of Ms. McPhee's book, in the temporarily relocated Middlesex County courthouse in a brand new, air-conditioned building in Woburn, Massachusetts. During the second week of the trial, outside temperatures there reached the mid-nineties. One male spectator even wore Bermuda shorts.

Rather than incur the expense of traveling to Woburn and staying in a hotel, I stayed at home in Nantucket, where ocean temperatures in the fifties kept the ambient air temperature a full ten degrees cooler than in Woburn, watched the webcast of the entire trial "gavel to gavel" on www.WHDH.com, the website of the Channel 7 NBC Affiliate in Boston, recorded each day's audio portion and downloaded it onto an MP3 device for subsequent private listening and note-taking, then deleted the files. (Other media outlets may also have carried the unified webcast of the trial. My attorney has indicated that a webcast of a public trial is itself in the public domain.) The presentation was excellently made, and on most days was divided into two horizontal screens side-by-side: one for the examining counsel, one for the witness. The district attorney called more than one hundred sixty witnesses. Each time the jury entered, the cameras scanned the ceiling — except early in the trial, when at least two jurors' faces appeared to have been inadvertently shown. Most of the time, the spectators' section of the small, low-ceilinged courtroom seemed to have several unoccupied seats.

    I am indebted to Classics Professor Emeritus Fred C. Mench of The Richard Stockton College Of New Jersey for proofreading the manuscript at various stages of its development, making helpful emendations, and keeping in check my instinctive sympathy for the underdog.

Michael Wells Glueck
Nantucket, Massachusetts
June-July 2008

Witnesses For The Prosecution

The defendant's parents and brother attended every session of the trial. Jury selection (known as the process of *voir dire*) occupied a typical four days, during which the defense exercised all of its challenges. One prospective juror was dismissed after revealing sentiments from others in the pool along the lines of "He's the fellow who murdered his family; fry him and send him away." Such comments redoubled attorney Weinstein's vigorous but unsuccessful efforts to convince the judge to authorize a change of venue, preferably to Edgartown on the cool and fashionable island of Martha's Vineyard.

The presiding judge was the Honorable Diane Kottmyer. District Attorney Michael L. Fabbri was the prosecutor, assisted by experts in DNA and computer science; Elliot M. Weinstein and Stephanie Page served as defense attorneys.

Mr. Fabbri portrayed the defendant as an unemployed electrical engineer overwhelmed by the financial burdens of renting a house for $2,700 per month, making lease payments on a white BMW X-3 van that had been repossessed from its previous owner, and otherwise providing for a new baby and a demanding, non-working wife who wished to live only in eastern Masschusetts (a requirement that forced Neil to decline an offer from a Silicon Valley company, Ross & Ross International). Entwistle, alleged the prosecutor, was dissatisfied with his sex life and surfed such websites as AdultFriendFinder.com, HalfPriceEscorts.com, and OneOnOneSex.com in search of alternative partners.

After seeking unsuccessfully to persuade the judge to question potential jurors about their attitudes toward visitors of such adult sex-oriented websites, and prevented by Massachusetts law from posing such questions themselves, the defense attorneys claimed that the Entwistle couple's guests had also used their laptop computer, and Weinstein in particular excoriated investigators for not examining it for fingerprints.

The lawyers for the defense eschewed an insanity defense, which would have entailed an implicit admission that their client caused the deaths in the case, and which is seldom successful. Such a defense failed utterly in the Nantucket murder trial of Thomas E. Toolan, about which I wrote a published account entitled *The Trial Of Thomas E. Toolan III*. Instead, perhaps borrowing a page from the O.J. Simpson double-murder trial, in the face of a mountain of incriminating forensic and DNA evidence Weinstein and Page built their case upon reasonable doubt. They could not, of course, identify or even suggest an alternative perpetrator, but they steadily probed perceived omissions in the state police crime laboratory's investigation. Why, for example, hadn't the Hopkinton house been searched for occult or hidden blood? The investigator's response that given the abundance of visible bloodstains he hadn't found it necessary to search the bathroom sink trap, toilet, or shower for occult blood was scornfully dismissed as a violation of his responsibility to be careful and thorough in his work. "Things aren't always what they seem" became the defense's mantra. With a straight face, Attorney Weinstein repeatedly assured the jury that Neil Entwistle loved his family deeply, and that they were blissfully happy. Surprisingly, prosecution witnesses – including Priscilla Matterazzo, Rachel's mother -- supported such assertions, adding that the couple loved and respected one another, and were friends as well as lovers, with no apparent friction. Such testimony, together with the fact that the newlyweds paid the equivalent of three months' rent up front, tended to cast doubt on the existence of a motive to commit the murders on the part of the defendant.

Whereas Mr. Fabbri sought substantive information from the police investigators, encouraging them to speak in full paragraphs, Mr. Weinstein and Ms. Page insisted upon advancing hypotheses that required only a "yes" or "no" answer from prosecution witnesses. On several occasions Judge Kottmyer interrupted Mr. Weinstein by ruling that the defendant being cross-examined at the moment was entitled to answer a question but needn't limit his answer to "yes" or "no." I suspect that Weinstein's sarcasm offended jurors; it clearly alienated a number of witnesses, at least one of whom began answering his "questions" with a dismissive "sure." To one persistently uncooperative witness, he remarked, "You know what? I don't want to ask you any more questions today. Thank you." To me, this attorney came across as occasionally acerbic but consistently cogent and effective, although a number of his hypotheses about various witnesses' activities struck them as flawed and elicited negative responses.

An aside: before the case had been assigned to a trial judge, Mr. Weinstein asked a judge at a preliminary hearing not only to release his client on bail but even to permit him to return to England and stay with his parents until the trial began. The judge denied this motion as unprecedented and unwarranted.

On the day of the murders, a college friend of Rachel's and her sister were expected for dinner at five o'clock. They arrived more than two hours late, having been unable to reach their hosts by telephone to advise them of the delayed arrival. Upon reaching their Hopkinton home, they found no one home and waited for the white BMW van to appear. When it didn't, the long-time friend eventually called police, who permitted her to walk the Entwistle's dog, Sally, then waited with her sister until the wee hours of the morning. At the trial, this constitutionally soft-spoken, nearly inaudible woman testified that Rachel had been very "mothering" to her at Holy Cross College, and that she would visit Rachel's room each afternoon and curl up on her bed to take a nap. In her late twenties and apparently single, she described an intense devotion to the family in general and to Rachel in particular. This witness was among twenty-four who were cleared of any suspicion after their DNA and fingerprints were compared with those found on the murder weapon, which had been returned to the Matterazzo's arsenal in Carver: the defendant's around the trigger, the adult victim's DNA on the muzzle, which had been held less than eighteen inches from her head and chest but directly against the infant's chest.

Neil Entwistle had been introduced to guns by Rachel's stepfather and his friends, including Rachel's uncle, Lloyd Cooke, and he proved to be an apt pupil, evincing a natural talent for target shooting with various types of weapons: a shotgun, rifles, revolvers, pistols. He knew where the guns and ammunition were kept at Rachel's parents' home in Carver – on the kitchen countertop, where any visitor to the house could see them -- and he had a key to their house. He had also visited Priscilla Matterazzo at her place of employment. So his explanations to police that he went to the Carver house but couldn't gain entry to leave a note, and that he didn't even know where Priscilla worked, were found wanting. And a fraud investigator for eBay testified that Neil Entwistle after opening several accounts had received numerous complaints from eBay customers who said they had not received merchandise purchased from him. These complaints dated from the weeks just prior to the killings in January 2006, and often the buyers received only partial refunds by reason of limited funds in the associated bank account, which, a bank official testified, carried overdraft protection that the defendant tried to exceed with ATM withdrawals on the day he fled to England.

During a video depicting the bodies of the slain females, who were shot at close range, Entwistle visibly wept. To paraphrase Hamlet, perhaps one may weep and weep and be a villain.

The jurors and audiences both physical and virtual were also barraged with visual and verbal images of the bullet-punctured, bloodstained clothing worn by the victims and of the other substances that they contained, including seminal fluid, sperm, and fecal matter. Each time, Judge Kottmyer reminded the jurors of their duty to put aside personal feelings, view all of the evidence no matter how distasteful, and consider it.

As the trial progressed, Attorney Weinstein sought to cast doubt on the ballistic and DNA evidence, which showed that the odds of the DNA samples found on the grip of the murder weapon belonging to anyone other than the defendant were one in trillions or quadrillions, i.e., far more than the population of the earth as officially tabulated from available records worldwide by the Federal Bureau Of Investigation. In a challenge to the identification of lead residue found at in the master bedroom with emissions from the murder weapon, he elicited admissions that that weapon was not specifically test-fired to determine how far it could project vaporous lead residue, and that the possibility of the defendant's DNA having been transferred onto the weapon from another surface could not be scientifically eliminated. Whether the jury will regard his efforts as grasping at straws remains to be seen, but the prosecutor immediately countered by eliciting details of the laboratory's sterility, the protective garments worn by the scientists, and the care with which evidence was collected and packaged.

The highlight of the DNA testimony concerning mixtures or fractional components of the defendant's and the victim's DNAs and bodily fluids came when the prosecutor's expert asked a female lab scientist the following: "Based on your knowledge and experience, is it unusual that a female would not be the major contributor to a sperm fraction?" Answer: "No, it would not."

On the twelfth day of the trial, the judge and counsels for prosecution and defense spent nearly an hour reviewing numerous documents pertaining to the defendant's accessing various websites; Her Honor admitted most by reason of their probative value, especially when the prosecution pressed, but excluded some others that the prosecution admitted were duplicative or because, being dated more than six months after the murders, their potentially prejudicial impact appeared to outweigh their probative significance. During this process, as indeed throughout the trial, all the attorneys were respecful and deferential toward the judge, accepting her decisions with professional aplomb. If the defense viewed some of those rulings as potential grounds for an eventual appeal, he expressed no such thoughts.

I found it interesting that the district attorney's office was able to use two software tools called n-CASE and NetAnalysis to retrieve the most recent three thousand logons, known as Index.DAT files, on the laptop. The machine in question, previously identified only as a laptop computer, was now specifically described as a Toshiba, hence a PC rather than a MAC. On my own PCs, in order to preserve privacy and security and to improve performance, I regularly empty the cache, erase the browsing history, clean up the hard drive, and delete the cookies in the Prefetch file. It would be instructive to learn whether the law enforcement agencies' software tools could undo or defeat such actions.

Not for the first time, I was struck by the wealth of resources available to the Commonwealth of Massachusetts. Many objective scientists had professionally analyzed various items of evidence painstakingly collected by the various police personnel and concluded that most of them tended to incriminate the defendant. None of them knew or held any personal animus against their subject. Cumulatively, however, their efforts seemed to be serving to build a cage around Neil Entwistle in which he would perforce spend the rest of his natural life. The defense could chip away at this mountain of evidence and cast doubt on some of its elements but seemed unable to provide convincing refutations.

A florist testified that Neil Entwistle called twice from London to order, first, a simple bouquet consisting of a single white lily coupled with one orange rose for his deceased daughter, Lillian Rose, and on the next day, assured that the credit card purchase had gone through, to order a sixty-dollar bouquet of assorted flowers for his late wife.

Two British friends of the defendant testified as to his disturbed and upset state upon his return to England. One said that he had visited his in-laws' home in Carver to obtain a gun with which to commit suicide, but had been unable to follow through, presumably because of the anticipated pain and suffering. Another said that the defendant had come to stay with him in London because British media were hounding his parents' home in Worksop, but that local police there had contacted him with a request to transmit to the defendant the urgent message that his presence was required back in Worksop so that he could be interviewed and monitored. Both agreed that the defendant's finances were in a perilous condition, and one mentioned that he reported that the Hopkinton house and BMW X-3 were purchased with, respectively, a mortgage and a loan, not rented or leased, and that Rachel had been eager to furnish every room of their home. But both testified that Neil described his marital relationship as harmonious; one of them laughingly allowed that he himself had had little success in affairs of the heart.

The friends also recounted Neil's version of the fatal events of January 21, 2006. He said he had traveled from the Hopkinton house, leaving the back door unlocked, to do some shopping at a nearby Staples store. When he returned, he continued, the back door remained unlocked, and nothing in the house appeared to have been disturbed until he entered the master bedroom and found the dead bodies of his wife and daughter. They expressed no skepticism about this story. One said that Neil told him he had called his mother-in-law as well as the police; this contradicts the police version, but may be only hearsay.

Then the prosecution's technical assistant called upon a state police computer expert, who testified that the Index DAT files retrieved from Neil Entwistle's Toshiba laptop showed that he had twice logged onto Google.com to conduct this search: "How to kill with a knife." One of the returns clicked on advised that one should aim for the aorta just below the rib cage and concluded with the hope that the article was informative and, especially, entertaining! The computer displayed three user log-ins – Ent, SrPub, and Contractor, and at least two of them had administrative privileges and were protected by passwords. The existence of a password did not seem insurmountable to me: I once forgot my administrator's password and was able to delete it completely without being able to read it, as it was encrypted with asterisks. Still, the probability that the defendant was the person who conducted such searches appeared overwhelming.

The judge immediately instructed jurors that they could consider all such technical evidence only with reference to the defendant's state of mind, motive, intent, and relationship with

Rachel, but not as proof that he commited the crimes alleged.

An attorney retained by the Quigs from whom Neil and Rachel had rented the Hopkinton house testified that he had contacted Neil to ask him whether he intended to return to the house and pay the past-due rent. If not, the attorney continued, he wished for Neil to collect his property. Neil replied that he did not plan to return to the U.S. and cared nothing for the property that he had left behind except for his late wife's jewelry. An arrangement was made for the attorney to collect and return the jewelry, but events intervened before this could be accomplished.

Then the DNA testimony resumed. As early as January 9, 2006 – twelve days before the killings – a user with the login ENT was using the Entwistles' laptop in the garage of their Hopkinton house to seek a cheap flight to London. Websites accessed for this purpose included those of airlines such as British Airways (BA.com) and travel agents such as LastMinute.com. Between that date and January 20, the ENT user was also accessing Monster.com and other job posting sites in search of a position, as well as a number of escort services' websites. From AdultFriendFinder.com he downloaded the profile of someone, presumably a woman, who had posted information about her availability on that site. One of the sites, found through the Google search engine, was local to Worcester, England and the user had downloaded Yahoo and Google maps of that area. Another sexually explicit site accessed was OneOnOnesex.com. A user with another login identified himself as an Englishman who was living in the U.S. and was seeking memorable one-on-one relationships with American "ladies," who, he said, he had been told and wished to confirm were "better in bed" than women "over the ocean." "We both want the same thing, so there is little point in dragging it out." How romantic!

At least one of the sites visited by a user with administrative privileges gave Neil Entwistle's name and U.K. address.

Then, with mounting excitement and triumph in his voice, the prosecution's computer expert asked the state police investigator who had analyzed that laptop's hard drive to read two entries from January 17. "What's he searching for, sir? What is Ent searching for?" Both were Google searches, and the defendant had clicked on a result for each. The items searched for were "knife in neck kill" and "quick suicide method." The implications for the defendant's state of mind were powerful and doubtless not lost upon the jurors, to whose imagination the nature of the results clicked upon defaulted in accordance with the judge's exclusion of such details as potentially inflammatory and prejudicial.

By conducting his cross-examinations carefully, Attorney Weinstein was careful not to open the door to the prosecution's reserve supply of incriminating documents not already introduced into evidence. He scored a point by demonstrating that a travel site visited in early 2006 had been searched for cheap fares for two adults without children for round-trip flights from Manchester, England to Boston on April 6 and back on April 18. Presumably Neil was considering bringing his parents over for a visit. Weinstein also demonstrated, not for the first time, that no police official or laboratory had tested any of the computers seized from Neil's home or his parents' home for fingerprints or DNA. But, taken as a whole, the first hours of testimony on this day, June 19, 2008, appeared devastating for the defendant's case.

A medical examiner testified that Rachel Entwistle had been five feet, two inches tall and weighed one hundred thirty-nine pounds at her death, while Lillian Entwistle had been twenty-two inches long and weighed about sixteen pounds. He said that the shot through Rachel's brain had killed her instantly, but that the shot through the lower quadrant of her left breast near the bottom had done little damage and was not debilitating. Lillian, he continued, bled to death within about one minute after the shot to her chest penetrated her liver and kidneys before exiting through her back. In order to determine the routes of the bullets, of course, he had performed autopsies, which in the case of Rachel's cadaver included shaving the top of the head and removing the scalp, skull cap, and brain. The privacy of murder victims ends along with their existence, and families have no say in the matter.

Cross-examination of this witness was conducted by Attorney Stephanie Page, who for the first time provided a window into the defense's real strategy: to demonstrate that the deaths of Rachel and Lillian Entwistle were, or plausibly could have been, a murder-suicide. Citing textbooks by Vincent and DiMaio and by Spitz and Fisher – prominent authorities in the field of forensic pathology, who have also published articles in scientific journals – Ms. Page elicited the following telling points from the doctor's testimony:

- Most people who commit suicide with firearms use handguns.
- Fully 72% of woman who commit suicide with firearms use handguns.
- Depression in general and post-partum depression in particular, which can last for a full year, are common causes of suicides by women.
- Many people who commit suicide with firearms shoot themselves more than once, and not all such shots prove fatal.
- Not all wounds of victims of suicide by gunshot are of the contact variety.
- While most people who kill themselves with a gun point at the temple, inside the mouth, or under the chin, it is not uncommon for the top of the head to be the chosen target.
- Even after inflicting a fatal wound upon himself or herself with a firearm, a person can sometimes still walk and move for a limited period of time.
- In only 29% of suicides do persons leave a note.
- In 39% of cases, a family member or friend moves the firearm after discovering the suicide.
- The bullet that killed Lillian Entwistle, who was being held with her back against her mother's breast, passed entirely through her body and entered the fatty tissue of Rachel Entwistle's breast, causing no serious damage.

- Rachel Entwistle had gunpowder residue on both sides of her two hands and could thus have shot herself in the top of the head, using both hands to steady the revolver.

After some prodding, the physician admitted that his report did not detail the exact path of each bullet fragment through Lillian Entwistle's body. Twice he retracted his answers by saying "I take it back," prompting a feisty Ms. Page to remark, on the first such occasion, "I'm glad you took it back," and, on the second, "You've taken a lot of things back today, Doctor." Both comments were objected to by the prosecution; the objections were sustained by the judge, who ordered the remarks stricken from the record. But the medical examiner admitted that "things are not always what they seem." He also acknowledged that he had not been told by police or prosecutor of the gunpowder residue on Rachel's hands, disagreed with the statement in *Spitz And Fisher's Medicolegal Investigation Of Death: Guidelines For The Application Of Pathology To Crime Investigation* that a pathologist needs to know about such matters in order to determine correctly the cause of death in cases involving fatal gunshot wounds, and denied that such information would have been helpful or even that he would wish it to have been provided. This clearly exasperated Ms. Page, who exclaimed "Oh my goodness!" and was again cautioned subtly by the judge, who ordered the remark stricken from the record. As Mae West famously remarked, "Goodness has nothing to do with it." Ms. Page then challenged the doctor's objectivity by asking,

"Whom do you work for, sir?"

"The Commonwealth."

"For whom do you testify?"

"The prosecution, usually."

The female attorney and the medical examiner also skirmished about whether, as Vincent and DiMaio claim in their book, *Forensic Pathology, Second Edition (Practical Aspects of Criminal and Forensic Investigations)*, pain receptors are located only in the skin. The attorney was attempting to show that Rachel's breast wound was not so excruciatingly painful as to have prevented her from firing a second shot into the top of her own head. The doctor disagreed, as did the prosecutor upon cross-examination, when he asked whether appendicitis attacks, coronary thromboses, or strokes cause pain to the subjects. The doctor answered in the affirmative, and his answer seems to jibe with common experience. Also under cross-examination, the physician claimed that the presence of gunpowder residue upon Rachel's hands showed only that she was in a room in which a firearm was discharged.

It is important to note that if the defense's postulated version of events proves sufficiently plausible to the jurors, they will have justifiable grounds to find reasonable doubt and acquit the defendant of the double murders with which he is charged. "Things are not always what they seem."

Police officers from the United Kingdom described how they had contacted Neil's friend, Dashiel Mundy, through his mobile telephone and met him at an underground train station, where they learned that Neil had boarded a train that had just left the station. The officers caused the train to be halted with the doors shut two stations down the line, drove there, and upon arrival, relying upon photographs and descriptions, recognized Neil sitting in the second car from the front. They then caused the engineer to open just one door opposite Neil's location, and placed their subject under arrest. There and at the Charing Cross police station, they confiscated items on his person and in a blue bag that he was carrying: a copy of the Sports News journal, a handwritten note with a telephone number, and a wallet containing nearly five hundred pounds sterling along with several credit cards, including one from PayPal. This occurred on February 6, 2006; nine days later, Neil was turned over to U.S. marshals for the flight back to the United States.

The same police also testified that they had visited Neil's parents at their Worksop home, from which they seized two desktop computers, one laptop computer, and a wallet containing seven U.S. dollars. All but the two sums of cash were produced in court. There was no explanation of the money's whereabouts, nor any testimony as to whether the newspaper contained personal advertisements, or whether the telephone number belonged to Dash or to an available woman who had listed herself in print or on a website. Attorney Weinstein elicited testimony from the British police officers that a metal ring belonging to the defendant had been seized from his blue bag. Weinstein also claimed that Neil had been wearing his gold wedding band at the time of his arrest. The Brits had no record at all of that item.

In the afternoon, jurors listened to a two-hour tape recording of two interviews in which Neil tearfully told a Massachusetts state trooper by telephone from his parents' home in Worksop that he had discovered the bodies of his wife and daughter, fatally shot in bed together, after returning home from doing errands. He said that he knew he should have called police but "just couldn't get it clear" in his head. Instead, he said, in a "trancelike state" he had flown to England and traveled to his parents' home the following day, soon recovering from his "trance" sufficiently to realize that he had "not done the right thing" by leaving the United States without first informing police or his wife's family. He claimed that he had considered committing suicide after finding the bodies but had been unable to do so because he knew "it would hurt."

Throughout the interviews, Neil repeatedly denied killing his wife and baby, saying "no, no, no" and "why would I do that?" The reiterated denials of guilt, recorded and presented by the prosecution, could not be challenged, as the defendant would have been through cross-examination had his attorneys elicited such statements from him after calling him to the witness stand, which during the playing of the recording was occupied by the state trooper who had interviewed Neil by telephone and recorded the conversation. Before the recording was started, Judge Kottmyer saw to it that the jurors were provided with transcripts, presumably anticipating that one or more of them might have difficulty in understanding Neil's British accent. But she instructed jurors that only what they heard Neil say constituted evidence – not the trooper's questions, and not the transcripts, which she indicated would not be available to them during their eventual deliberations.

In the interview, Neil said that he had driven to a nearby Staples store to buy a wireless router for his laptop so that he could use it upstairs rather than just in the basement where it was wired to a modem. He'd located the item, he said, but decided to compare Wal-Mart's price before buying it, then got lost and couldn't find Wal-Mart's. He then went to a Starbuck's and bought and consumed two lattes, charging them to his credit card, then returned home, discovered the bodies lying on the master bed, and covered them with the bedclothes. He then drove, he continued, to his in-laws' house in Carver for the purpose of obtaining a gun with which to shoot himself but couldn't gain entry because he found that the extra key normally kept with the car keys wasn't in its usual place; he thought that it might have been taken by Rachel. This was consistent with the defense's theory of a murder-suicide by Rachel, but significantly the conversation occurred before Neil had been arrested, charged, and provided with legal representation, i.e., before the defense had developed and coordinated its version of how the deaths of Rachel and Lillian occurred. Then, he said, he tried to find Priscilla's office but failed, as he had never driven there himself. He drove around, bought gasoline with a credit card, went to Boston's Logan airport, left and drove around some more, then returned to the airport. There has been no testimony as to where he slept that night, so tbat question remains unanswered. In any event, on the next day he flew to London's Heathrow Airport, as is clear from his account as well as from credit card records. But his alibi is shaky: nothing purchased at Staples, hence no receipt from that source, and no known credit card purchase of gasoline. What remains potentially damning is the following set of facts: that he didn't call 911, police, or the Matterazzos; that he fled to England; and that he considered suicide, which the police interviewer clearly viewed as a sign not of extreme distress but of guilt. Even after arriving in England, Neil failed to call his in-laws, leaving the task to his father, who spoke with them for a few moments from the family home on Coleridge Road in Worksop (a town in the Bassetlaw district of Nottinghamshire, England on the River Ryton at the northern edge of Sherwood Forest, Robin Hood country) and then put Neil on the telephone.

On Monday, June 23, 2008, yet another recorded interview of Neil by the Massachusetts state trooper, conducted by long-distance telephone, was played for the jurors. The trooper, now a sergeant, indicated that the keys to the house in Carver were on the BMW keys found in the Hopkinton home, and Neil described the key chain and the colors of the BMW and Hopkinton house keys that it held. This contradicts, of course, Neil's statement in the first interview that he neither had nor could find a key to the Carver house. And on this day he repeated that statement. Also, the fact that the guns were returned to Carver not only further contradicts these statements but throws doubt on the defense's murder-suicide theory, since Rachel certainly could not have returned them after the fact. If Neil had returned them, of course, then he needn't have gone to his in-laws' home to obtain a gun with which to commit suicide, since the gun would have been right in front of him.

Neil did ask the trooper how quickly his wife and daughter died, and was assured that their deaths were quick, their suffering brief and limited.

Curiously, Neil told the trooper that he had extracted a kitchen knife from the block with the intention of committing suicide, but that the anticipated pain had stopped him, and so he had replaced it. This is a somewhat different version from the story that he had told his friend: then he said that he was considering making his quietus with the Matterazzo's twenty-two caliber revolver, but couldn't do so.

During this interview, one of the cameras panned to Neil's parents and brother, who looked extremely anguished. The testimony seemed especially disturbing to his father. Even the judge, who was comparing the transcript with the audible testimony, looked rather grim.

Upon the conclusion of this witness' testimony, both sides rested! The defense called no witnesses. No one – not even Rachel's friend and confidante, Joanna Gately – took the stand to testify that she seemed depressed at any time.

Closing Arguments

A bench conference concerning the judge's charge or instructions to the jurors is taking place; then closing arguments will be made; then the judge will read the instructions before the jury retires to consider its verdict.

But – the judge has asked Neil Entwistle to stand while she poses some questions to him. "You shouldn't read anything into the questions as to what you should do." Attorney Weinstein quickly asked if the interview could be held in chambers. "Yes, of course." There the questions were posed privately, in conference, with only the prosecuting and defense attorneys present.

Since there is no evidence of any intent on the part of the defendant to cause maximum pain, there will be no charge to the jury about atrocity or extreme cruelty in this case. Nor will there be an instruction about involuntary manslaughter, as the evidence doesn't support it. Jurors will have a variety of possible verdicts, including second-degree murder, to consider. The jurors will also be instructed not to consider the failure of the defendant to testify as an indication of guilt. But, they will be instructed, they have a duty to return a verdict of guilty of the highest charge proved by the Commonwealth beyond a reasonable doubt.

Her Honor admonished jurors not to take notes except to jot down the numbers of any exhibits referenced during closing arguments, and then Attorney Weinstein gave the defense's closing arguments.

He emphasized that the investigators assumed that Neil was guilty; that Neil didn't mention finding and returning the twenty-two caliber revolver on the bed during his interviews or call 911 because of his unwillingness to implicate Rachel in the murder-suicide; that Neil's main concern during the interviews was to protect Rachel. He emphasized the gunpowder residue on Rachel's hands, noting again that the medical examiner had not been informed of that fact, reconstructed his theory of the murder-suicide in some detail, emphasizing that the weight of the revolver forced Rachel to hold it in both hands, and stressed reasonable doubt. He accused the prosecution of failing to prove a negative: that Rachel did not fire the fatal shots. The fitted bedsheet around Rachel's hands, he continued, were not examined for gunpowder residue, which might have proved the prosecution's case had the tests been made. The failure to make such probative tests, he continued, constituted reasonable doubt.

Why would Neil murder his wife and daughter, Mr. Weinstein asked? Because he visited internet sex sites? How many millions of people do that every day? And, one might add editorially, how many husbands and wives enhance their sexual experiences with one another by fantasizing that they are making love to some other persons whose images they have seen online or elsewhere?

This argument, too, seemed curiously at odds with previous testimony: the defense attorney had taken pains to emphasize that no one had tested Neil's laptop computer for fingerprints or DNA evidence. It appeared to be a concession that it was indeed Neil Entwistle who had visited the x-rated websites.

Concerning the timeline, the credit-card receipt from Starbuck's showed that Neil bought the two lattes there at 11:30 A.M. Upon arriving home, he went to the basement computer and looked for job information. At l2:31 P.M., he went upstairs and looked at Lillian's photograph. Could he have done this if he had just murdered her and Rachel? The defense averred that such callousness was impossible. Neil found the bodies, knew instantly what had happened, drove to Carver and returned the revolver. He couldn't tell the Matterazzos or the police what he knew, but needed to be with his family. If the gunpowder residue on Rachel's hands is worthy of jurors' consideration, then that is sufficient reasonable doubt to acquit the defendant. Joanna Gately's extreme concern, which caused her to sit outside the Hopkinton house in her car on a cold winter night, was for Rachel's state of mind. Only she knew that Rachel was depressed.

Attorney Weinstein declared the following:

- The burden of proof of guilt is upon the prosecution, which didn't check Joe Matterazzo's alibi or consult Rachel's doctors, who may or may not have been willing to provide them with confidential patient information.
- Neil had no plan, no luggage, no cash, no preparations to fly to London, only an understandable impulse to be with this family in England.
- The medical examiner worked for the prosecution and was not objective.

The defense attorney went on in this vein for half an hour, repeating the mantra that "Things are not always what they appear to be" and the desired verdict of not guilty as charged. Neil, he continued, was a computer engineer; if he knew that he was guilty and had to cover his tracks, he would have taken the laptop to England, or removed the hard drive, or destroyed its contents. Why, he asked rhetorically, is there no motive? Why had Neil no cash in his pocket? The investigators weren't fair to Neil or to jurors, who must perform the work of investigating the murder-suicide since the police did not do that. "Please do not compound this tragedy by finding Neil Entwistle guilty. He did not do this."

Then District Attorney Fabbri began his summation by agreeing that the burden of proof is on the prosecution. Pathologists Spitz, Fisher, and DiMaio, he continued, were not in the courtroom. He agreed that "things are not always what they appear," but gave as an example the testimony that the Entwistle's were a loving family with no problems. He reminded jurors of the murderous and salacious contents of the computer searches, and of the January 20th "job interview" that had been cancelled two days earlier, unbeknownst to Rachel.

Then Mr. Fabbri attempted to demolish the gunshot residue argument: only four particles on Rachel's hands out of "thousands" dispersed in a cloud of dust and vapor resulting from the discharging of the firearm. He insisted that this defense argument is "a red herring," that Rachel and Lillian were killed in the positions in which they were found. If Rachel were the shooter, he said, she would have obtained the gun days before, on January 16th, before the January 17th internet searches for ways to kill with a knife.

Rachel, he averred. was happy: back home, with her home, car, family, and, she thought, a loving husband. The argument that she was <u>frustrated by not being able to have unrestrained</u>

sex in the Carver home is not a reason for suicide. It makes no sense to attempt suicide by shooting through another person, or for Rachel, holding her baby, to have used both hands to shoot herself in the head at a distance of at least six inches. The scene itself suggests that what happened was not a suicide according to the defense theory; if it were, it would look different. Again, he said, Rachel had no motive to commit suicide.

What was Neil's reason to commit double murder? Sometimes there is no apparent cause or motive, but Neil, he suggested, was closing his wife and daughter out of his life, searching online for sexual partners, praising the beauty of one of the women whom he contacted. "I'm currently in a relationship, but I'm looking for more fun in the bedroom. What happens later we will not discuss now." The prosecutor asked rhetorically, "What does that say about his love and devotion for his wife." Why did Neil interrogate his wife about her relationship with a former classmate? Wasn't he projecting his situation – no job, blood relatives, friends – upon Rachel? Neil, Mr. Fabbri declared, had reached the tipping point and planned the double murder.

In the last few days at the Matterazzo home, the prosecutor continued, Neil was upstairs on the computer, searching for sexual partners as well as jobs, while Rachel and her parents played with Lillian. Addressing the defense's claim of negligence on the part of investigators in not examining the laptop for fingerprints, he said that Rachel had no time to search online for such things; she was planning the move to Hopkinton.

Neil, Mr. Fabbri declared, is an experienced traveler and knows how to buy a ticket without going to the counter at the last moment.

Then the prosecutor urged jurors to handle the revolver and consider how a five-foot-two-inch woman could have used it. He reminded them that Neil's DNA was all over the grip of the gun, Rachel's only on the large muzzle. The evidence, he noted, is that Rachel had no interest or experience in guns, and may not have even known how to load the revolver.

"I have no interest in this anymore" – Neil's recorded voice on a call to a friend in the United Kingdom – meant that he no longer had interest in his home, family, or possessions, the prosecutor declared. Yet he told the trooper interviewing him by long-distance that he needed to be with his parents. There are two sides to Neil Entwistle, the prosecutor insisted. Soon after arriving in England, Neil acquired a lot of cash and a cell phone, and told his friends a different story from what he had told the state trooper.

From London to Worksop the distance is one hundred twenty miles, but Neil put eight hundred miles on the rental car, and didn't arrive at the Worksop family home for thirty-six hours, not the two or three that it would have taken him to drive there directly from Heathrow Airport. He told a friend that he had no plans to return to the United States.

Mr. Fabbri emphasized the thoroughness, objectivity, and accuracy of the police's thorough investigation, which kept coming back to one place: the platform in the London underground station with a stopped train from which Neil was seeking, according to U.K. police, an open exit.

One person is responsible for these murders, the prosecutor continued, and he is sitting right over there: the man who pulled the trigger twice. "Consider the evidence thoroughly," he concluded, "and I'm confident that you will conclude that this was a homicide by a husband against his family and will find Neil Entwistle guilty of the dual murders."

Upon the conclusion of Mr. Fabbri's closing argument, the judge reminded jurors that what the attorneys say is not evidence, then called a one-hour lunch recess, after which instructed the jurors on applicable law and remanded the case to them for due consideration. One expert opined that in a circumstantial case such as this one a jury could require one to three days to reach a verdict.

The Verdict

Twelve jurors deliberated a day and one-half; four alternates continued to be present in case one or more of them was required to replace an active member. But that did not occur. After lunch on Wednesday, June 25, their foreman indicated to the bailiff that a verdict had been reached.

There were four counts, two of murder, two of possession (of a firearm and of ammunition). The following dialogue ensued:

Bailiff: "Foreperson of the jury, have you reached a verdict?"

"Yes."

"With respect to Count One of the indictment: How say you, Foreperson? 'Guilty' or 'Not guilty'?"

"Guilty of murder in the first degree of Rachel Entwistle."

"With respect to Count Two of the indictment: How say you, Foreperson? 'Guilty' or 'Not Guilty'?"

"Guilty of murder in the first degree of Lillian Entwistle."

"With respect to Count Three of the indictment: How say you, Foreperson? 'Guilty' or 'Not guilty'?"

"Guilty as charged."

"With respect to Count Four of the indictment: How say you, Foreperson? 'Guilty' or 'Not guilty'?"

"Guilty as charged."

The bailiff then repeated the four guilty verdicts and inquired:

"So say you, Foreperson?"

"Yes."

"So say you all?"

In perfect unison: "Yes."

The Sentence

Her Honor publicly thanked the jury for their service, noting its importance as well as the fact that not a single juror had asked to be excused despite economic hardships and family responsibilities. After asking the jurors to wait briefly in their room and then discharging them, the judge set sentencing for ten o'clock the following morning. She then exited the courtroom to speak privately, albeit briefly, with the jurors — no doubt to tell them that she agreed with their verdict and applauded their thoroughness.

On the next day, Prosecutor Fabbri asked that the two mandatory sentences of life imprisonment without possibility of parole be imposed consecutively, and the defense requested that they be imposed concurrently.

Then Priscilla and Joe Matterazzo, hand in hand, were permitted to come forward and address the court. Priscilla recounted the hardships of losing both a daughter and a granddaughter, and requested consecutive life sentences for the defendant. Joe addressed Neil directly, reproaching him for his choice of a defense strategy that impugned Rachel's memory and honor by accusing her upon no evidence whatever of having committed both murder and suicide. Implicitly, this criticism also appeared to be directed at the defense attorneys.

Then Rachel's brother — accompanied by his wife and a number of friends — was permitted to approach the bench. As might be expected, he bewailed the loss of a sister and niece for himself and his wife and of an aunt and cousin for his children, and then he, too, requested consecutive life sentences.

The judge asked whether Neil Entwistle wished to speak; Mr. Weinstein replied in the negative. No apology, certainly no admission of guilt, was forthcoming.

Then Judge Kottmyer responded by saying that while she understood the poetic justice of the requests for two consecutive life sentences, she was concerned that complying with those requests would create the false impression, especially abroad, that parole was possible in this case. "But it isn't. Absent a pardon by the Governor, Mr. Neil Entwistle will spend the rest of his natural life in prison. Thus consecutive sentences would be merely symbolic."

The jurist then announced the sentences that would be imposed: for the murders, two concurrent terms of life imprisonment at the maximum-security Cedar Junction prison in South Walpole, Massachusetts; for the charges of possession of a firearm and of ammunition, ten years' supervised probation, also to be served concurrently. She recounted the fees incident to such probation: sixty-five dollars per month for probation, and one victim-witness fee of ninety dollars. That added up to seven thousand, eight hundred ninety dollars. How the defendant – who had never found in his adopted country of the United States of America a job that was suitable both geographically and professionally, and whose prison earnings, if any, would be measured in cents per hour – was expected to be able to pay such assessments was not explained.

Attorney Weinstein asked if he might approach the bench "before final imposition of sentence," and Her Honor assented. The ensuing discussion, attended also by the prosecutor and defendant, was brief and private.

Then the bailiff repeated the sentences, and Neil Entwistle was led away, though not yet in handcuffs or shackes. He remained in the custody of the sheriff of Middlesex County for one more night, and on the next day he was sent directly to a maximum-security prison – but not the one specified by Her Honor. Rather, Massachusetts prison administrators assigned him to the Souza-Baranowski prison in Shirley, Massachusetts – an institution named for two officials who in 1972 were killed at the Norfolk penitentiary during an aborted escape attempt by a convicted murderer. This choice of penal institution seems grimly appropriate when one remembers that Rachel's maiden name was Souza.

Aftermath

Outside the courthouse, Neil's parents spoke with members of the press. His mother, Yvonne, averred that she "knew" that Rachel had been depressed and committed first the murder of Lillian and then suicide, and bemoaned her son's prison sentence. Neil's father, Clifford, vowed to work tirelessly to clear his son's name.

Joe Matterazzo spoke briefly, thanking the public for its outpouring of support through letters and cards.

Then the prosecution team congratulated one another upon the diligent work that had produced convictions on all counts.

And Mr. Weinstein maintained that there were substantial grounds for appeal: the judge's denial of a change of venue; the absence of fingerptint and DNA testing of the laptop computer seized as evidence.

It will probably take at least a year before an appellate court decided the automatic appeal of the first-degree murder convictions. If either side appeals that decision, then the matter will be sent to the Supreme Judicial Court of the Commonwealth for possible consideration. The chances of a reversal appear slim, indeed.
******

Here are subsequent and significant developments:

02/08/2012	NOTICE of April argument sent.
03/08/2012	ORDERED for argument on April 6. Notice sent.
04/06/2012	Oral argument held.
08/14/2012;	RESCRIPT (Full Opinion): Judgment affirmed. (By the Court)
09/11/2012	RESCRIPT ISSUED to trial court.
11/19/2012	Notice: Certiorari petition filed in U.S. Supreme Court.
01/17/2013	Notice: Certiorari denied by U.S. Supreme Court.

Satiric Epitaph:

My name was Neil Entwistle.

I learned to use a pistol

I hid it in the thistle,

Beneath an old epistle.

I shot my wife and daughter,

Although I hadn't oughter,

And left them as bug fodder.

Flew home to ma and pater.

To Boston extradited,

"An intruder" I recited.

Convicted by a jury,

I pass my days in fury.

Denied just like a plain tort.

I claim that I'm not guilty,

Do even parents believe me?

Photographic and Audio Exhibits

For photographs of Neil, Rachel, and Lillian, please visit this URL:

http://graphics.boston.com/bonzai-fba/AP_Photo/2006/02/09/1139491777_8480.jpg

www.ingramcontent.com/pod-product-compliance
Lightning Source LLC
Chambersburg PA
CBHW021940170526
45157CB00005B/2366